DRAGTAILS

FIERCE COCKTAILS INSPIRED BY DRAG ROYALTY

DRAGTAILS

FIERCE COCKTAILS INSPIRED BY DRAG ROYALTY

GREG BAILEY & ALICE WOOD

ILLUSTRATIONS BY
RUTH MOOSBRUGGER

WHITE LION
PUBLISHING

CONTENTS

FOREWORD

Libation is defined as a drink poured out as an offering to a deity.

Drag and a good libation go hand in hand. One in the hand can be the perfect accessory to a look. It can be comforting to hold as one saunters through a dark, crowded nightclub, or sipped flirtatiously as you attract others into the narrative of your style and presence. Its flavours can be familiar and comforting, since we have our 'usual' and favourites. Sometimes its presentation can punctuate the aesthetic, depending on the vessel it is served in. It's why the cocktail dress exists; slight formality intended to appeal and possibly to strike up conversation. It is the ultimate elixir in social settings.

A good drink can provide confidence and unleash inhibitions, or be used as a tool to take a performance to another level of elegance or irreverence. It is something I almost always have to brighten the experience and add to the armour of my anxieties. Drag, after all, is armour, and a good cocktail is the plumed helmet and, in some instances, the sword.

Over the decades of doing drag, my taste in cocktails has evolved according to my interests at that current time. It's still evolving. Whisky in my Rock and Roll phases; a Tom Collins or Martini when I wanted to feel like a vintage pin-up; absinthe for its ritual when I felt goth; a Moscow Mule or Mimosa for a cheery brunch. These days my preference is mostly for cold Sauvignon Blanc; it feels light and engaging and has become my signature. I admit that in my earliest years, drinking alcohol wasn't as nuanced and special as it is now. Chugging cheap was my preferred method of numbing, choosing gluttonous consumption to make me seem much more outgoing than I actually am. False bravado to combat shyness, many times with regret to follow. As I've grown and matured, so have my tastes. Nowadays, drinking a cocktail is festive and celebratory. It heightens the mood and vibe, it feels special and intentional. Instead of numbing, it now tickles all of the senses, feeling playful rather than punishing, and I am looking forward to being tickled by all the dragtails in this book.

A dear friend loves to tell the story of when I was getting ready for an event. As I pieced my look together and placed all the details, I could see it all coming together while I preened in the mirror and felt myself awaken. Bit by bit, the transformation from chrysalis to butterfly was taking place. When I thought I was finished, I gave it a once-over and sighed. Something felt incomplete. I looked around me to find the missing piece, the exclamation mark. My friend presented me with a cold cocktail made with my favourite spirits. I took a sip and said to myself 'Now, I'm in drag'.

RAJA GEMINI

DRINK AND DRAG

INTRODUCTION BY **GREG BAILEY**

DRAGTAILS: when said out loud you could be forgiven for thinking that this would be a book of short stories from or about drag performers, but you would be mistaken. This is actually a well-crafted and curated collection of cocktail recipes inspired by some of the world's most fascinating drag artists. Yet, maybe you're not mistaken. I like to think of this book not just as a recipe book to teach you how to mix up the campest of cocktails, but as a book of stories, a compendium that gives an insightful yet fun look into the glorious and ever-growing world of drag. Within these pages, you'll find cocktails inspired by some of the world's most fashion-forward drag artists (such as Raja Gemini, Tayce and Bimini Bon Boulash), drinks dedicated to unique drag oddities (Juno Birch, Katya, Ginny Lemon and Meatball), beverages inspired by filth and horror drag artists (the Boulet Brothers, Divine and Landon Cider), cocktails concocted for glamour queens (Danny La Rue, The Vivienne and Nicky Doll, to name just a few) and even a boozy shake inspired by a bodybuilding drag Barbie (Miss Toto).

So why drag-inspired cocktails? Is there a correlation between drag and drink? Well, if you want to suck the fun out of it you could say that, historically, a drag performer is simply a commodity to increase alcohol sales at your local bar. The more entertaining the performer is, the more people will frequent the establishment, meaning more alcohol sales! There you go, there's the correlation. But that's not really it, is it? That's like comparing a drag performer to the sad old fruit machine you see in that run-down pub on the corner of your road, and we should give a queen more dignity than that, surely?

Nowadays, the link between drag and cocktails has never been more apparent than at drag-themed brunches. Where once if there was a drag queen present at breakfast it would have been after an all-nighter – wig in her bag, comfies on, and baseball cap pulled down low hiding the half-sweated-off beat – but drag is now a staple even in traditionally heteronormative venues. Born from queer spaces like the famous American drag-themed burger restaurant chain Hamburger Mary's, historical British LGBTQ+ pubs and countless international drag-centric queer spaces the world over, drag brunch is the dinner theatre of the LGBTQ+ scene. Slap bang between breakfast and lunch (who are we kidding, it's an all-day affair really) you'll find a gaggle of fabulous drag performers ready to entertain you while you eat your poached eggs and smashed avocado on toast, all while you are supplied with bottomless pitchers of your favourite cocktails. Now, I wouldn't be a very good cocktail and drag enthusiast if I didn't encourage you to drink responsibly, not only for your own well-being but also for any drag artist who's there to entertain you. So, for the happiness and sanity of all drag brunch performers the world over, I would encourage anyone who is going to their first drag brunch to remember; don't get too loud or heckle the drag performer (you'll never live it down, and will probably end up on social media because of it), don't touch the drag performer (yes, they have lovely hair, but just no, babe!), and lastly the stage is not yours, it's the drag artist's (so stay in your seat and enjoy the show).

Now I may have had a couple of glasses of the Cara Melle-inspired *Drunk in Love* cocktail on page 68, but you're my friend and I love you. No really, I do, I love you, I'm not just saying that, so I'm going to get all meaningful and tell you the deeper correlation between drag and mixology. It lies in the creativity and expression that both a drag artist and a mixologist has. They both have the unique ability to excite, delight and bring joy to the person who is consuming what they create. But even that is just scratching the surface of what this union really is; it goes further than simply being a consumer. Whether you are the consumer, creator or enthusiast, drag can bring an unparalleled level of freedom through self-expression that is seldom felt in the world. It gives you a chance to relax and let go of your worries... much like the Laganja Estranja-inspired cocktail *Chilled Greens* on page 62, Mawma!

Beyond these pages of beautiful illustrations and recipe suggestions, you'll find the crossover of drink and drag goes even deeper. Drag artists the world over are turning their hand to creating their own alcohol brands, such as Joe Black's limited edition Decopunk gin, Shea Couleé's collaboration with Goose Island beer, Shea Coul-Alé, and Raja Gemini's Sauvignon Blanc, 'Wine and Complain'. Much like the varying tastes and qualities of all the different cocktails and alcohol varieties in the world, no drag performer is the same. Some are sweet like a Daiquiri, some are complex like the Boulevardier and some are as bitter as a grapefruit gin and tonic. You'll get a taste of everything in this book. If, however, you don't drink alcohol, we're not suggesting you need to break your sobriety to have a camp old time. Where we've been inspired by a drag performer who happens to be sober, we have suggested an equally delicious mocktail version of the cocktail. Be creative and use this book as an inspirational starting point to create your own flamboyant fusions. Whether you choose to add alcohol or not, mixology and drag are for everyone to enjoy.

So whether you fancy a quiet night in watching *To Wong Foo, Thanks for Everything! Julie Newmar*, or you're getting ready for a night out at Drag Bingo, why not grab some glasses and your cocktail shaker and get in the mood with a drag-inspired cocktail with your best Judies?

THE SHOWGIRL

INSPIRED BY **DANNY LA RUE**

A true legend of drag, the embodiment of high camp, Danny graced countless theatres over their 60+ year-long career, not to mention numerous TV and film appearances. Danny was one of the most glamorous drag performers the world had seen, with marabou feather plumage to rival that of any Vegas showgirl and costumes fit for a big-budget Tinseltown musical. This classic Vodka Cranberry has an unusual zing of lime juice and a feathery soft frothy top created by adding an egg white at the mixing stage. Finally, for even more glamour and camp, it is adorned with a vibrant maraschino cherry.

INGREDIENTS

25ml (⅞fl oz) vodka

25ml (⅞fl oz) lime juice

50ml (1⅔fl oz)
cranberry juice

1 egg white

To serve

Maraschino cherry

METHOD

Pour the vodka, lime juice, cranberry juice and egg white into a cocktail shaker with ice. Shake vigorously for 20 seconds.

Strain into a chilled coupette glass and top with a maraschino cherry to serve.

VERY DELTA

INSPIRED BY **DELTA WORK**

Delta Work, a killer lip-syncer, podcaster, Emmy award-winning hair and wig stylist and West Hollywood legend, is – to anyone who knows her, or simply follows her on social media – the queen of autumn and winter. She preps for spooky shows and celebrations months in advance, but as soon as that last trick or treater has taken that final piece of Halloween candy, Delta is moments away from decking the halls and cracking out the festive finery. For the lover of the colder months, we suggest finishing this spiced warm drink with some indulgent whipped cream, dusting it with ground cinnamon and adding a cinnamon stick. This cocktail is Very Delta.

METHOD

Pour the espresso, pumpkin spice syrup and bourbon or dark rum into a heatproof glass or mug.

Heat the milk in a heatproof jug in the microwave or in a saucepan, until steaming. Whisk the milk until frothy and pour into the glass or mug. Finish with a topping of whipped cream, a dusting of ground cinnamon and a cinnamon stick to serve.

INGREDIENTS

1 shot (30ml/1fl oz)
of espresso

15ml (½fl oz)
pumpkin spice syrup

25ml (⅝fl oz) bourbon
whiskey or dark rum

200ml (6¾fl oz) whole milk

To serve

Whipped cream

Ground cinnamon

Cinnamon stick

QUEEN OF SCOTS

INSPIRED BY **LAWRENCE CHANEY**

Lawrence Chaney is much like the Loch Ness Monster... a Scottish legend. Making their debut on the Glaswegian drag scene, Lawrence quickly became one of Scotland's rising stars of drag, cementing this by winning the crown on *RuPaul's Drag Race UK*, season 2. We couldn't just serve you Vodka and Irn-Bru, so we decided to roll with Lawrence's signature colour purple and fun personality to form this big, bold, beautiful beverage that'll make you want to say bing, bang, bong!

INGREDIENTS

50ml (1⅔fl oz) vodka

25ml (⅚fl oz) blue Curaçao

100ml (3⅓fl oz) cranberry juice

25ml (⅚fl oz) juice from a jar of maraschino cherries

Lemonade, to top up

To serve

Maraschino cherry

METHOD

Pour the vodka, blue Curaçao, cranberry juice and maraschino cherry juice into a hurricane glass full of ice and stir.

Top up with lemonade and finish with a maraschino cherry to serve.

IS SHE THIRSTY?

INSPIRED BY **HUNGRY**

Hungry is Björk's makeup artist... That should paint a pretty good picture of the sort of drag artist Hungry is. There is a real organic beauty to what Hungry creates, but the sort of beauty you'd find maybe in the insect world. Turning the heads of the fashion elite firmly in their direction, Hungry's artistry mimics organic symmetry with knife-edge precision, transforming themselves or whoever is lucky enough to be in front of their brush into mesmerising floral transmutations. With its unusual flavour of violet, cut through with the sharpness of lemon juice and the botanical bitterness of gin, this cocktail is the perfect ode to this otherworldly drag artist.

INGREDIENTS

15ml (½fl oz) crème de violette

15ml (½fl oz) lemon juice

25ml (⅝fl oz) gin

To serve

Lemon twist

METHOD

Pour the crème de violette, lemon juice and gin into a cocktail shaker with ice. Shake vigorously until combined.

Pour the mix into a chilled martini glass and top with a lemon twist.

PIÑARITA

INSPIRED BY **MANILA LUZON**

You can't create a book of drag-inspired cocktails without including Manila Luzon! She's appeared on so many franchises of *Drag Race* it's hard to keep up, but with an acute appreciation and love of camp it's understandable why she keeps coming back to grace our TV screens. Manila has injected so much joy into *RuPaul's Drag Race* and pop culture in general – with looks inspired by Big Bird, the Teletubbies, a bondage bunny, and Bob Ross – but it's her affinity with the pineapple that has birthed some truly memorable looks for Manila. So, it's only fitting to dedicate this cocktail not only to Manila but to all other pineapple fanatics.

METHOD

Pour the tequila, pineapple juice, triple sec and lime juice into a cocktail shaker with ice and shake vigorously until combined.

Take a rocks glass and squeeze and rub a lime wedge around the rim of the glass and then dip the rim in salt. Pour the mixture into the glass and finish with a pineapple wedge.

INGREDIENTS

50ml (1⅔fl oz) tequila

50ml (1⅔fl oz) pineapple juice

25ml (⅚fl oz) triple sec

25ml (⅚fl oz) lime juice

To serve

Lime wedge

Salt, for the glass

Pineapple wedge

BALTIMORE MUD PIE

INSPIRED BY **DIVINE**

A drink inspired by the filthiest woman alive was always going to be dripping in the brown stuff... we mean chocolate, of course! Starting as an icon of the underground in Baltimore, going on to become an art-house mega star and forever the muse of the pope of trash, John Waters, Divine embodies the outrageous rebellion in all of us and this cocktail had to do the same, pushing the boundaries of taste and decadence – this cocktail had to be NAUGHTY. The thick, creamy, velvety creation is poured into a hurricane glass splattered with drizzles of chocolate sauce then topped with lashings of whipped cream, grated chocolate and a maraschino cherry.

METHOD

Place the vodka, Irish cream liqueur (liquor), crème de cacao, chocolate ice cream and ice into a blender and blend until combined.

Drizzle chocolate sauce inside a hurricane glass and pour the cocktail mix into the glass. Top with whipped cream, grated chocolate and a maraschino cherry to serve.

INGREDIENTS

30ml (1fl oz) vodka

30ml (1fl oz) Irish cream liqueur (liquor)

30ml (1fl oz) crème de cacao

2 scoops of chocolate ice cream

1 scoop of ice

To serve

Chocolate sauce

Whipped cream

Grated chocolate

Maraschino cherry

ABSOLUTELY ALIEN

INSPIRED BY **JUNO BIRCH**

This absolutely stunning, out-of-this-world drag icon of Manchester, and internationally renowned Sims obsessive is never seen without her manicured Marigolds, and very rarely without her signature specs. But it's Juno's uniqueness, off-kilter wit, and 1960s wardrobe that makes her stand out from the crowd... Okay, maybe it's the blue skin too. When trying to embody an alien drag queen who is trying to blend in with the human race (but failing miserably) into a cocktail, we decided to take the classic Gin and Lemonade and make it stick out like a sore thumb – by turning it blue and pink.

INGREDIENTS

15ml (½fl oz) blue Curaçao

100ml (3⅓fl oz) lemonade

25ml (⅝fl oz) pink gin

To serve

Maraschino cherry

METHOD

Pour the blue Curaçao and lemonade into a rocks glass full of ice and mix well.

Top up with the pink gin and finish with a maraschino cherry to serve.

LIVERPUDLIAN BUBBLY

INSPIRED BY **THE VIVIENNE**

'Girls, are you sick of guzzling loadsa water and still feeling drier than me granny on a Saturday night?!' Well, come here and try our cocktail inspired by Liverpool's finest, The Vivienne! You should be drippin'... in diamonds while necking this classy cocktail. Pop to the offie and grab yourself a bottle of Champagne and Angostura bitters, then fetch your finest champagne flute... this is the perfect start to a night on the town.

INGREDIENTS

1 sugar cube

2–3 dashes of Angostura bitters

Squeeze of lemon juice

Champagne, to top up

To serve

Lemon twist

METHOD

Place a sugar cube in the bottom of a Champagne flute. Add the Angostura bitters and a squeeze of lemon.

Top up with Champagne and finish with a lemon twist.

TIP For a mocktail version, omit the Angostura bitters and try substituting the Champagne for a non-alcoholic sparkling wine.

LATE-NIGHT SNACK

INSPIRED BY **MEATBALL**

We could have drawn inspiration from their time on season 1 of *The Boulet Brothers' Dragula*, or their hilariously entertaining club acts, but we thought there was no better way to embody this incredible queen in a drink than to draw inspiration from how they garnered their name, which was from their need of late-night meatball subs after countless nights out while living in NYC! There's no need to walk to Nino's Pizza for a meatball sub – with this cocktail you can turn your last drink of the night into your pre-bed meal.

METHOD

Put the vodka, beef stock, tomato juice, lemon juice, horseradish sauce, Worcestershire sauce, Tabasco sauce, black pepper and salt in a cocktail shaker with ice and shake vigorously until combined.

Strain into a rocks glass filled with ice and finish with a celery stick, pickles and olives.

INGREDIENTS

60ml (2fl oz) vodka

60ml (2fl oz) beef stock

60ml (2fl oz) tomato juice

15ml (½fl oz) lemon juice

½ tsp horseradish sauce

3 dashes of Worcestershire sauce

4 dashes of Tabasco sauce

2 grinds of black pepper

1 pinch of sea salt

To serve

Celery stick

Pickles

Olives

MINTY FRESH

INSPIRED BY **PEPPERMINT**

A sugary-sweet confection and a New York City drag legend. Choosing her drag name because her college crush loved peppermints was certainly a great way to get that person's attention. Peppermint has garnered so many impressive titles over the years – including actress, singer, songwriter, Broadway star and activist – that it's now her accolades demanding your attention, not just her name. That being said, she in fact couldn't have picked a better name for herself: she's joyous, sweet and strong, much like her crush's festive favourite candy (and this drink).

METHOD

Pour the vodka, crème de menthe, Irish cream liqueur (liquor) and single cream into a cocktail shaker with ice. Shake vigorously until combined.

Pour the mix into a chilled martini glass and top with a mint sprig.

TIP For a mocktail version, try substituting vodka for a non-alcoholic vodka alternative, crème de menthe for a mint syrup and use extra cream to replace the Irish cream liqueur.

INGREDIENTS

25ml (⅚fl oz) vodka

25ml (⅚fl oz) crème de menthe

25ml (⅚fl oz)
Irish cream liqueur (liquor)

15ml (½fl oz) single cream

To serve

Mint sprig

DARK CABARET

INSPIRED BY **JOE BLACK**

A rich, raucous, heavy breath of times gone by; the essence and energy of a 1920s' Weimarian cabaret, the glamour of a 1940s' Marlene Dietrich, and with a rasp in his voice akin to that of Tom Waits; Brightonian drag oddity Joe Black casts his dark allure over the contemporary drag scene. Invoking the spirit of Joe, the coupette glass is first rinsed in absinthe, creating the perfect hedonistic starting point for this devilish creation with its heady blend of complex flavours. And with a nod to Art Deco lavishness, it's topped with a dark cherry.

INGREDIENTS

Absinthe rinse

25ml (⅞fl oz) sweet vermouth

50ml (1⅔fl oz)
rye or bourbon whiskey

2 dashes of Angostura bitters

To serve

Dark cocktail cherry

METHOD

Pour the absinthe into a coupette glass and swirl
it around to coat the inside of the glass.
Discard the excess absinthe.

Pour the sweet vermouth, whiskey and Angostura
bitters into a mixing glass with ice and stir to combine.
Strain the mixture into the coupette glass and top
with a dark cocktail cherry.

THE VAUDEVILLIAN

INSPIRED BY **JINKX MONSOON**

Aesthetically, Jinkx Monsoon is a quirky mix of eras and moments in history. She's an old soul; a red-headed Vaudevillian, pagan witch with impeccable comedic talents, and an *Absolutely Fabulous* 'cool mom' demeanour. No wonder she made history by becoming the first ever drag queen to be cast in the role of *Chicago*'s Mama Morton on Broadway. Taking reference from her seasonally stormy last name and inspired by Jinkx's uniqueness, this cocktail is crafted in her honour. Punchy ginger beer, ginger syrup and lime juice are accompanied by the unusual herbal flavours from the Angostura bitters. Add the soulful taste of dark rum and this drink is as unique and mysterious as Jinkx herself.

INGREDIENTS

25ml (⅚fl oz) lime juice

5ml (⅙fl oz) ginger syrup

150ml (5fl oz) ginger beer

2 dashes of Angostura bitters

50ml (1⅔fl oz) dark rum

To serve

Lime wedge

METHOD

Pour the lime juice, ginger syrup, ginger beer and Angostura bitters into a tall collins glass and mix.
Add ice to the glass and top with the rum.
Add a lime wedge to serve.

TIP For a non-alcoholic version, omit the Angostura bitters and substitute the rum for cola.

PAINT THE TOWN BLUE

INSPIRED BY **BLU HYDRANGEA**

Are you ready to paint the town blue? Raise a glass to the Northern Irish Queen of the mothertucking world! From the first ever cast of queens of *RuPaul's Drag Race UK*, season 1 to the winner of the first cast of queens on *RuPaul's Drag Race UK vs the World*, Blu is an exceptionally talented makeup artist, costume designer and performer. Blue being her signature colour and her name, there was no other way to go with this ode to Miss Hydrangea.

METHOD

Pour the Irish whiskey, blue Curaçao and lime juice into a cocktail shaker with ice and shake vigorously until combined.

Pour the mix into a hurricane glass filled with ice and top up with lemonade. Stir to combine and top with a maraschino cherry to serve.

INGREDIENTS

25ml (⅞fl oz) Irish whiskey

25ml (⅞fl oz) blue Curaçao

25ml (⅞fl oz) lime juice

Lemonade, to top up

To serve

Maraschino cherry

GRAND MAHA-RAJA

INSPIRED BY **RAJA GEMINI**

With a deep understanding and a wealth of lived experience in both the drag and the fashion worlds, Raja easily predicts and influences the future of drag, pulling from her past and proud Indonesian heritage to do so. Raja is the embodiment of style and indulgence; she exudes opulence and is a devout maximalist, yet has a calming aura of earthly wisdom and practises a holistic way of living. This duality is a classic trait of her Zodiac sign Gemini and is mirrored in the slightly chaotic energy that the sambuca brings to this cocktail. Its heavy tang of anise sits alongside the citrus in the lemonade, blending with the rich brandy and Grand Marnier. With a nod to Indonesian flavourings, a cinnamon stick adds more complexity and warmth when left to infuse.

INGREDIENTS

25ml (⅝fl oz) sambuca

25ml (⅝fl oz) Grand Marnier

15ml (½fl oz) brandy

100ml (3⅓fl oz) lemonade

To serve

Cinnamon stick

METHOD

Pour the sambuca, Grand Marnier, brandy and lemonade into a rocks glass full of ice. Place the cinnamon stick in the glass and stir to infuse.

AMARULA QUEEN

INSPIRED BY **SHEA COULEÉ**

She didn't come to play, she came to slay. Shea Couleé is the video vixen of Chicago – she's strutted down the runway for Fenty, shot campaigns for Valentino and was the winner of *RuPaul's Drag Race All Stars,* season 5. Adding beautiful historical and cultural references into her looks, Shea's drag is a love letter to black women the world over. Paying homage to Shea and her gorgeous celebration of African culture, this deep, rich, silky smooth chocolate cocktail incorporates the uniquely African flavour of the marula fruit by combining Amarula cream in the mix.

INGREDIENTS

15ml (½fl oz) dark crème de cacao

25ml (⅚fl oz) vodka

50ml (1⅔fl oz) Amarula cream

3 dashes of chocolate bitters

Cocoa powder, for dusting

METHOD

Pour the crème de cacao, vodka, Amarula cream and chocolate bitters into a cocktail shaker with ice. Shake vigorously until combined.

Pour the mix into a chilled martini glass and finish with a dusting of cocoa powder.

AFTERNOON TEA

INSPIRED BY **VICTORIA SCONE**

She was scone too soon from her season of *Drag Race UK*, but she came back to slay on *Canada vs the World*! Victoria Scone is the first AFAB queen to be cast on any franchise of *RuPaul's Drag Race*, and she proves it doesn't matter what's between your legs; any gender identity can be a drag queen... just make sure you have Charisma, Uniqueness, Nerve and Talent! This cocktail leans into Victoria's very British chosen surname, with lashings of cream and an abundance of strawberry flavours that accompany a scone so well, taking the concept of cream tea to the next level!

INGREDIENTS

25ml (⅝fl oz) rum

25ml (⅝fl oz) Irish cream liqueur (liquor)

12.5ml (⅖fl oz) strawberry syrup

1 scoop of strawberry ice cream

To serve

Whipped cream

Sliced strawberries

METHOD

Put the rum, Irish cream liqueur (liquor), strawberry syrup and strawberry ice cream in a blender and blend until smooth.

Pour the mix into a rocks glass and top with whipped cream. Finish with sliced strawberries to serve.

QUINCE CHARMING

INSPIRED BY **CHEDDAR GORGEOUS**

Intrigued? I think you will be. You may have only heard of Cheddar Gorgeous from her very memorable stint on *RuPaul's Drag Race UK*, season 4, but much like the iconic British landmark she's named after, she's actually been around for a very, VERY long time. We believe Cheddar wasn't born, but simply emerged from a lake or cave one day, an alien deity of sorts who eventually found her way to the Manchester drag scene. From her name, you probably wonder what this cocktail could be. Surely it won't be cheddar flavoured?! But what's wrong with cheese, Cathy? Everybody likes a fondue from time to time. But no, it's actually flavoured with quince! And what pairs gorgeously with the sophistication of quince? Cheddar, of course!

INGREDIENTS

½ tsp honey

25ml (⅞fl oz) quince vodka

25ml (⅞fl oz) port

Chilled fizzy apple juice,
to top up

METHOD

Put the honey, quince vodka and port in a champagne
flute and stir to combine.

Top up with chilled fizzy apple juice to serve.

THE SHADY LADY
INSPIRED BY **BIANCA DEL RIO**

'Well, well, well! I hope you bitches are ready!' Because this cocktail is going to be as delicious as Bianca reading a queen to filth. If you're a fan of drag and you're not familiar with Bianca Del Rio, then quite frankly you should be ashamed of yourself. Starting out as a Cher impersonator, she quickly realised that corner of the market was over-saturated and threw herself fully into comedy, becoming a fixture of the New Orleans and New York City club scenes. Bianca is the first drag queen to headline Carnegie Hall and Wembley Arena, she's an incredible performer, costume designer, insult comic… and inexplicably has a voice that is indistinguishable from the sound of a car slipping out of gear.

INGREDIENTS

25ml (⅚fl oz) lime juice

1 passion fruit

2 tsp caster sugar

50ml (1⅔fl oz) cachaça

To serve

Lime wedge

METHOD

Place the lime juice, passion fruit pulp and sugar into a rocks glass and muddle until the sugar has dissolved.

Pour over the cachaça and stir to combine.

Top with crushed ice and add a lime wedge to serve.

TIP For a mocktail version, try substituting the cachaça for ginger ale.

BLOOD SACRIFICE

INSPIRED BY **THE BOULET BROTHERS**

Hello, Uglies! Want a cocktail that embodies drag, filth, horror and glamour? Then look no further, as we've got a treat for you. Take some fresh pig's blood, the eyes of a salamander and the tears of your enemies, mix them together and you've got a cocktail that Dracmoda or Swanthula would be happy to serve at a Boulet Brothers' soiree. Okay, okay, it's vodka, creme de cassis and cranberry juice, with a lychee and black olive garnish... We wouldn't want you to experience the true Boulet Brothers extermination fantasy, now would we?!

INGREDIENTS

25ml (⅝fl oz) vodka

25ml (⅝fl oz) creme de cassis

50ml (1⅔fl oz) cranberry juice

To serve

Black olive

Lychee (peeled and destoned)

METHOD

Pour the vodka, creme de cassis and cranberry juice into a cocktail shaker with ice and shake vigorously until combined.

Pour the mix into a chilled martini glass. Push a black olive into the centre of a lychee and place in the drink to serve.

NEON ANGEL
INSPIRED BY **DETOX**

Let's re-toxify with this dedication to the living mannequin herself... Detox! This cocktail is as crisp as her Mugler-esque silhouette, as neon bright as her love of the 80s, and even plays with some of the top notes from her favourite Angelic perfume, leaving you feeling like you've just been enveloped in her scented wake. If you wanted a drink that personifies Detox, then you've had it! OFFICIALLY!

INGREDIENTS

25ml (⅞fl oz) white rum

25ml (⅞fl oz) blue Curaçao

25ml (⅞fl oz) pineapple juice

Lemonade, to top up

To serve

Maraschino cherry

METHOD

Pour the white rum, blue Curaçao and pineapple juice into a cocktail shaker with ice and shake vigorously until combined.

Pour the mix into a highball glass filled with ice, top up with lemonade and finish with a maraschino cherry to serve.

CREAM-A BALLERINA

INSPIRED BY **BROOKE LYNN HYTES**

Don't let the name fool you, this incredible drag performer is not from the neighbourhood in Brooklyn, New York, but is Canadian to the core. Brooke Lynn Hytes trained with the National Ballet School of Canada, travelled the world as a principal ballerina with Les Ballets Trockadero de Monte Carlo, won the highly coveted crown and title of the Miss Continental drag pageant, was a *RuPaul's Drag Race* finalist, and is now host of *RuPaul's Drag Race Canada*; Brooke Lynn is a drag juggernaut and as iconic in the drag world as the maple leaf is in Canada. With a tip of our Mountie hat to the queen of true north, a rocks glass is filled with crushed ice and a combination of Irish cream liqueur, Amaretto, cream and – of course – a hearty splash of maple syrup.

INGREDIENTS

50ml (1⅔fl oz)
Irish cream liqueur (liquor)

25ml (⅝fl oz) Amaretto

25ml (⅝fl oz) single cream

5ml (⅙fl oz) maple syrup

METHOD

Pour the Irish cream liqueur (liquor), Amaretto, single cream and maple syrup into a cocktail shaker with ice and shake vigorously until combined.

Fill a rocks glass with crushed ice and pour over the mix to serve.

THE TENSION TAMER

INSPIRED BY **COCO PERU**

Are you bothered? Do you need your tensions tamed? Well, this take on a Long Island Iced Tea will certainly do that for you. With countless 'one-woman shows', numerous film and prime-time TV appearances, plus interviewing icons such as Bea Arthur, Liza Minnelli, Lily Tomlin and Jane Fonda, Coco Peru is a living drag legend of the queer community. But it's this Los Angeles-dwelling Bronxite's fondness for a relaxing cup of tea and her obsession with her homegrown Californian lemons that have inspired this cocktail.

METHOD

Put the lemon vodka, gin, tequila, rum, triple sec and lemon juice in a highball glass with ice. Stir to mix.

Top up with cola and finish with a lemon slice to serve.

INGREDIENTS

12.5ml (⅖fl oz) lemon vodka

12.5ml (⅖fl oz) gin

12.5ml (⅖fl oz) tequila

12.5ml (⅖fl oz) rum

12.5ml (⅖fl oz) triple sec

12.5ml (⅖fl oz) lemon juice

Cola, to top up

To serve

Lemon slice

KING OF KINGS

INSPIRED BY **ADAM ALL**

Specs-tacular king of kings, Adam All, brings a unique blend of neon nerdcore and suave sophistication to the galaxy of drag. With that in mind, we thought this cocktail should simply be a twist on a classic. A tart and distantly saccharine spike of marmalade rests on the heady flavours of the bourbon whiskey. The uncomplicated but confident method is testament to Adam's satirical take on modern manhood.

METHOD

Place the marmalade, Angostura bitters and a splash of water into a rocks glass and mix until combined.

Fill the glass with ice and pour over the whiskey. Stir for about 30 seconds. Top with the orange peel to serve.

INGREDIENTS

1 tbsp marmalade, slightly heated

2–3 dashes of Angostura bitters

50ml (1⅔fl oz) bourbon whiskey

To serve

Strip of orange peel

CHERRY ON TOP

INSPIRED BY **CHERRY VALENTINE**

Cherry made quite the impact on season 2 of *RuPaul's Drag Race UK*, with a gorgeous, dark glamour to her drag, beyond perfect makeup skills, and one of the best laughs you'll ever hear. Cherry grew up in the UK Romani community, which historically sticks very rigidly to the gender binary. This can cause real anguish to LGBTQ+ individuals who grow up within the community. Cherry was, whether she intended it or not, a shining beacon of positivity to fellow LGBTQ+ Romani individuals and to anyone growing up queer in a family or community that aren't as accepting as they should be. So please raise a glass to the memory of one Miss Cherry Valentine.

METHOD

Pour the cherry vodka and cherry syrup into a highball glass filled with ice. Top up with cola and stir to mix.

Finish with a black cherry to serve.

INGREDIENTS

50ml (1⅔fl oz) cherry vodka

15ml (½fl oz) cherry syrup

Cola, to top up

To serve

Black cherry

CHILLED GREENS

INSPIRED BY **LAGANJA ESTRANJA**

'Oh, y'all wanted a twist, 'ey?' With countless catchphrases and -isms, Laganja Estranja is one of the most quotable queens who's ever graced *RuPaul's Drag Race*. Laganja changed the game for drag performers the world over, making the 'Death Drop' the most notable and staple dance stunt in a drag performer's arsenal. But it's Miss Estranja's namesake and the reason she's so cool, calm and collected (when she's not feeling VERY ATTACKED) that has inspired this cocktail, so grab the CBD and let's get medicated, Mawma, because if it's not green, we're not interested!

METHOD

Pour the tequila, triple sec, green juice, lime juice, sugar syrup and CBD into a cocktail shaker with ice and shake vigorously until well mixed.

Take a rocks glass and squeeze and rub the lime wedge around the rim of the glass and then dip it in salt. Pour the drink into the glass and top with a lime slice to serve.

INGREDIENTS

50ml (1⅔fl oz) tequila

50ml (1⅔fl oz) triple sec

50ml (1⅔fl oz) green juice

15ml (½fl oz) lime juice

15ml (½fl oz) sugar syrup

3 drops of CBD oil

To serve

Lime wedge

Salt for the glass

Lime slice

TERMINALLY DELIGHTFUL

INSPIRED BY **BENDELACREME**

DeLa for short, De for shorter, Ms Creme if you're nasty! But nasty she is not; the best of the best, the terminally delightful BenDeLaCreme is the perfect mix of showgirl aesthetics and comedic genius. She made history by eliminating herself while being the front-runner on *RuPaul's Drag Race All Stars,* season 3, staying true to herself by creating her own rules! This drink could have easily strayed into the realms of punk due to the pretty punk move DeLa made on the show, but instead it's a classic, pretty in pink but with a distinct twist that makes it stand out from the crowd.

INGREDIENTS

50ml (1⅔fl oz) vodka

25ml (⅚fl oz) triple sec

25ml (⅚fl oz) cranberry juice

10ml (⅓fl oz) lime juice

To serve

Orange twist

METHOD

Pour the vodka, triple sec, cranberry juice and lime juice into a cocktail shaker with ice and shake vigorously until combined.

Pour the mix into a chilled coupette glass.
Finish with an orange twist to serve.

NEWPORT SUPERMODEL

INSPIRED BY **TAYCE**

The cheek, the nerve, the gall, the audacity and the gumption! We've only gone and made a cocktail to encapsulate the stunningness of the lip-sync assassin of *RuPaul's Drag Race UK,* season 2. This concoction is as red as the Welsh Dragon, and as unique as Tayce herself. We suggest sipping this cocktail while wearing a killer red custom body suit, poker-straight blonde hair to your waist and fake blood sprayed across your face, while listening to 'Memory' by Elaine Paige to really feel the full fantasy.

INGREDIENTS

50ml (1⅔fl oz) spiced rum

50ml (1⅔fl oz) blood orange juice

25ml (⅚fl oz) lime juice

15ml (½fl oz) sugar syrup

3 dashes of Angostura bitters

To serve

Blood orange slice

METHOD

Pour the spiced rum, blood orange juice, lime juice, sugar syrup and Angostura bitters into a cocktail shaker with ice and shake vigorously until combined.

Pour the mix into a chilled rocks glass and serve with a blood orange slice.

DRUNK IN LOVE

INSPIRED BY **CARA MELLE**

Burlesque Queen B, Atlanta Peach living in London, Cara is the 'Yoncé twin with *Drag Race* fandom. With live vocals and flawless choreo, Cara Melle is a goddess on stage and can captivate an audience with simply a look. She gives you diva, she gives you strength, she gives you power, and much like Beyoncé herself, she shows you how to run the world. Poured into a sleek martini glass with an added pinch of sea salt, this cocktail is sweet, salty and sticky if you're nasty!

INGREDIENTS

25ml (⅞fl oz) salted caramel vodka

25ml (⅞fl oz) coffee liqueur

25ml (⅞fl oz) espresso coffee

To serve

3 coffee beans

Pinch of sea salt

METHOD

Pour the salted caramel vodka, coffee liqueur and espresso coffee into a cocktail shaker with ice and shake vigorously until combined.

Pour the mix into a chilled martini glass. Finish with coffee beans and a sprinkle of sea salt to serve.

RUSSIAN DOLL

INSPIRED BY **KATYA**

Yekaterina Petrovna Zamolodchikova... dare you to say THAT three times quickly after a few of these robust cocktails! This queen makes 'kooky' look boring and will always keep you on your toes with her irreverent wit and debatable fashion choices. She can get her leg behind her head quicker than you can say 'The United Socialist Soviet Republic', and just like Katya, this cocktail is fruity, sharp and strong. Throw in a few 'THWORPS' for good measure and you're ready to go!

INGREDIENTS

25ml (⅝fl oz) vodka

25ml (⅝fl oz) cherry liqueur

25ml (⅝fl oz) cranberry juice

To serve

Maraschino cherry

METHOD

Fill a rocks glass with ice and add the vodka, cherry liqueur and cranberry juice. Stir to mix. Top with a maraschino cherry to serve.

TIP For a mocktail version, try substituting the vodka and cherry liqueur for a non-alcoholic vodka alternative and cherry juice.

FANCY A SLICE?

INSPIRED BY **GINNY LEMON**

'Fancy a sliiice?!' You can almost hear Ginny's infamous catchphrase with every sip of this twist on a classic Sour. The queen of Worcester is known for being camper than Christmas and always clad in sunshine, and this cocktail is exactly that! The tart gin and lemon give way to the velvety maple syrup to create a texture fit for a pantomime dame.

INGREDIENTS

25ml (⅚fl oz) gin

15ml (½fl oz) maple syrup

50ml (1⅔fl oz) lemon juice

To serve

Lemon slice

METHOD

Fill a rocks glass with ice and add the gin, maple syrup and lemon juice. Mix to combine.

Top with a lemon slice to serve.

PASH MY PEACH

INSPIRED BY **COURTNEY ACT**

If everyone is relying on ugly, why can't Courtney rely on being pretty?! Let's be honest though, Miss Act isn't just relying on her looks. She's an Aussie powerhouse who can dance with the stars and sing like an idol. But yes, Courtney knows how to do sexy, and strewth this is a bloody sexy drink! Mix it, top it up with prosecco and a peach slice, then grab yourself some Chapstick, mascara and a good rooting wig, and you're set for a bloody good night.

INGREDIENTS

25ml (⅚fl oz) peach schnapps

50ml (1⅔fl oz) peach iced tea

Prosecco, to top up

To serve

Peach slice

METHOD

Pour the peach schnapps and peach iced tea into a champagne flute. Top with prosecco and finish with a peach slice to serve.

POISONED APPLE

INSPIRED BY **LANDON CIDER**

It's no secret that the drag community is sadly laden with misogyny everywhere you turn, so working for years to carve out a place for themselves in such a male-dominated scene is not only impressive, it's revolutionary. Landon Cider not only brings hope for other drag kings and cis-gender females working within the drag scene, but also brings hope to anyone who is marginalised in the community. Landon's historic win of *The Boulet Brothers' Dragula*, season 3, left a deliciously refreshing taste in everyone's mouth, and this spiced apple ode to the King of Filth, Horror and Glamour will certainly do the same.

INGREDIENTS

25ml (⅞fl oz) spiced rum

50ml (1⅔fl oz) cloudy apple juice

25ml (⅞fl oz) cranberry juice

To serve

Red apple slice

METHOD

Fill a rocks glass with ice and add the spiced rum and cloudy apple juice. Mix to combine.

Top with the cranberry juice and finish with a slice of red apple to serve.

SPONGE QUEEN

INSPIRED BY **MONÉT X CHANGE**

You know what they say: Monét changes everything! And the sponge queen herself, Monét X Change, certainly did. Monét has competed on three different iterations of *RuPaul's Drag Race*, won a place in the *Drag Race* Hall of Fame, launched and hosted her own chat show called *The X Change Rate*, and is an incredibly talented bass opera singer. But rather than drawing on Monét's many talents, this cocktail has been created with a visual approach, soaking up some inspiration from one of Monét's most memorable looks... that sponge dress! This yellow and green layered drink will leave you feeling ready to clean up any competition.

INGREDIENTS

25ml (⅝fl oz) Malibu

150ml (5fl oz) pineapple juice

5ml (⅙fl oz) sugar syrup

15ml (½fl oz) blue Curaçao

METHOD

Fill a rocks glass with ice and add the Malibu and 100ml (3⅓fl oz) of the pineapple juice. Mix to combine.

In a separate jug, mix together the remaining pineapple juice with the blue Curaçao. Gently pour the mixture over the back of a spoon into the glass to form a green layer.

HEAD OVER HEALS

INSPIRED BY **PANGINA HEALS**

Drag Race Thailand co-host and *RuPaul's Drag Race UK vs the World* contestant Pangina loves the idea of unity, so she took inspiration from the supercontinent Pangaea when forming her own drag name. The idea of unity is deepened further by blending Pangaea with one of her favourite drag artists, Ongina. But it was Pangina's surname that interested us most when creating this cocktail. Drag has had a healing effect on Pangina in her everyday life, so she decided to adopt this word to finalise her drag name. Thai basil, the key ingredient in this cocktail, is rich in antioxidants, and supposedly has anti-cancerous, antiviral, anti-bacterial and antifungal properties, so our Pangina-inspired cocktail really could have the ability to heal!

INGREDIENTS

7 Thai basil leaves

50ml (1⅔fl oz) gin

15ml (½fl oz) lime juice

5ml (⅙fl oz) sugar syrup

METHOD

Place 6 of the Thai basil leaves into a cocktail shaker and muddle. Add ice to the shaker and pour in the gin, lime juice and sugar syrup. Shake vigorously until combined.

Strain into a chilled coupette glass and top with the remaining basil leaf to serve.

AZUSA IDOL

INSPIRED BY **ADORE DELANO**

Who's ready to PARTY!? No need to ask Adore
Delano, she IS the party. This Libra's address is
Hollywood and she's all about fun, music and
living life exactly how she wants to. Adore is the
personification of a smoky, low-lit dive bar with
a jukebox in the corner playing Nirvana or The
Distillers. Her style is a cool mix of icons like Stevie
Nicks, Joan Jett and, of course, a touch of Brody
Dalle. Adore's cocktail is inspired by the classic Jack
'n Coke that you'd expect any rocker to be knocking
back, but we've turned the amp up to 11 by adding
the chaser shot of tequila straight into the glass.
NOW you're ready to party!

INGREDIENTS

25ml (⅞fl oz) Jack Daniel's

15ml (½fl oz) tequila

Cola, to top up

To serve

Lime wedge

METHOD

Fill a rocks glass with ice and add the Jack Daniel's
and tequila. Top up with cola and stir to combine.

Finish with a lime wedge to serve.

PAINT STRIPPER

INSPIRED BY **LILY SAVAGE**

Fling open the doors of any gay pub in 1980s' London, and through the wall of cigarette smoke, Joop aftershave and stale beer, you'd find a bejewelled queen upon the stage, with the look of a Hollywood starlet and the mouth of a docker. And none are more iconic than Lily Savage. Lily won over not only the pub-goers, but also the British public, becoming a household name into the 1990s, with her leopard-print wardrobe, unmistakeable northern rasp, and humour so blue she could make a sailor blush. This cocktail is just like the late, great Lily: potent, smoky and not for the faint of heart!

INGREDIENTS

Scotch whisky rinse

50ml (1⅔fl oz) vodka

10ml (⅓fl oz) dry vermouth

To serve

Green olive

METHOD

Pour the Scotch whisky into a martini glass and swirl it around to coat the insides of the glass. Discard the excess whisky.

Pour the vodka and dry vermouth into a cocktail shaker with ice and shake vigorously until combined. Pour the mix into the martini glass. Top with a green olive to serve.

PB AND SLAY

INSPIRED BY **RUPAUL**

RuPaul Andre Charles has shaped and expanded the drag community to lofty heights that 10+ years ago very few could have predicted. Countless albums, TV shows franchised the world over, international conventions and even chocolate bars; RuPaul is an LGBTQ+ mogul, and certainly is the Willy Wonka for a whole generation of drag queens. So how do you create a cocktail that perfectly encapsulates this guRu of a generation? Well, you start with one of the most profound lyrics a RuPaul song has to offer... 'Uh huh. Oh yes, honey. Due to the fact that her thighs spread just like P-nah p-nah p-nah, p-nah, peanut butter!'

METHOD

Spread the peanut butter into a small bowl and dip the rim of a rocks glass into the peanut butter. Spread the grated chocolate into another bowl and dip the rim of the rocks glass in to coat the peanut butter. Fill the glass with ice.

Put the vodka, crème de cacao, cream and pinch of salt in a cocktail shaker with ice and shake vigorously until combined. Pour the mix into the glass to serve.

TIP For a mocktail version, try substituting the vodka and dark crème de cacao with chocolate milk.

INGREDIENTS

1 tbsp smooth peanut butter

1 tbsp grated milk or dark chocolate

25ml (⅞fl oz) vodka

25ml (⅞fl oz) dark crème de cacao

50ml (1⅓fl oz) single cream

Pinch of salt

WHAT'S HER NAME?

INSPIRED BY **PRIYANKA**

The first-ever winner of *RuPaul's Drag Race Canada*, what's her name?... PRIYANKA! Energy at 100 and always peppy, it's no wonder she was a successful children's TV presenter and household name in her previous career. How do you capture that energy in a cocktail? Ah yes, a twist on an espresso martini will work nicely. Taking inspiration from Priyanka's Indo-Guyanese ancestry and her love of Bollywood (she shares a name with Bollywood legend Priyanka Chopra, after all), this cocktail injects some chai spice and star anise into the mix. For sweetness, there's maple syrup (a Canadian staple), creating a drink that perfectly embodies Canada's first-ever drag superstar.

INGREDIENTS

50ml (1⅔fl oz) vanilla vodka

25ml (⅝fl oz) Kahlua

25ml (⅝fl oz) chai tea, cold

25ml (⅝fl oz) single cream

5ml (⅛fl oz) maple syrup

To serve

1 star anise

METHOD

Pour the vanilla vodka, Kahlua, chai tea, single cream and maple syrup into a cocktail shaker with ice and shake vigorously until combined.

Pour the mix into a chilled martini glass.
Finish with a star anise to serve.

LOUISIANA DREAMGIRL

INSPIRED BY **CHI CHI DEVAYNE**

Stepping onto our TV screens back in 2016, Chi Chi won our hearts with her cheerful Louisiana charm and her bright outlook on life. Her memorable time on season 8 of *RuPaul's Drag Race* taught her, and us, that 'it doesn't matter where you're from, that has nothing to do with how far you can go. Never be ashamed of how you walk, talk, because that is going to be the key to your success.' Drag lost a truly beautiful soul when Chi Chi passed away in 2020, so we'd like you to join us and raise a glass to the country queen, the dream girl, Chi Chi DeVayne. 'Laissez les bons temps rouler!'– *Let the good times roll.*

METHOD

Fill a highball glass with ice and add the Pimms, lemonade and 7up. Stir to combine. Finish with a cucumber slice to serve.

INGREDIENTS

25ml (⅝fl oz) Pimms

75ml (2½fl oz) lemonade

25ml (⅝fl oz) 7up

To serve

Slice of cucumber

RED VELVET

INSPIRED BY **LADY RED COUTURE**

Hello, children. Are you ready for some cutting up and kiki-ing? Are you ready for a gay old time? Well, I hope you are because now it's time to celebrate the legend that is Lady Red Couture! Lady Red was a pillar of the Los Angeles drag community, literally! She was 6ft 7in, and 7ft 2in in heels! She had a commanding stage presence with her infectious personality and her impressive vocal range. She was kind, caring and nurturing, and known for helping aspiring drag queens learn to sew, do makeup and perform. It's no wonder she garnered the name of Mother Couture. As a tribute to Lady Red, this drink is her signature colour, velvety sweet, with a dusting of sparkles. So, raise your glass and let's all say 'HEY QWEEN!'

INGREDIENTS

25ml (⅞fl oz)
raspberry vodka

25ml (⅞fl oz)
white (clear) crème de cacao

25ml (⅞fl oz) cranberry juice

1 egg white

To serve

Edible red glitter dust

METHOD

Pour the raspberry vodka, crème de cacao, cranberry juice and egg white into a cocktail shaker with ice and shake vigorously until combined.

Pour the mix into a chilled martini glass and sprinkle with edible red glitter dust to serve.

HOT PEACH

INSPIRED BY **CHORIZA MAY**

With probably the funniest and most self-deprecating entrance lines in any *RuPaul's Drag Race* franchise, Choriza May simply slapped us in the face with her comedic identity with one poignant sentence: 'Don't hate me 'cause I'm beautiful, hate me 'cause I'm an immigrant.' What's her story, you may ask? Originating from Spain, Choriza is Newcastle's spiciest, meatiest and silliest sausage. With over-the-top flamboyant costumes that the campest of matadors would be jealous of, and a debut song entitled 'My pussy is like a peach', Choriza certainly knows how to make a lasting impression, and this spicy jalapeño and peach concoction will do just the same!

INGREDIENTS

1 peach, de-stoned

25ml (⅝fl oz) tequila

15ml (½fl oz) lime juice

15ml (½fl oz) sugar syrup

2 pickled jalapeño slices

To serve

Lime wedge

METHOD

Place the peach, tequila, lime juice, sugar syrup and jalapeño slices in a blender with 6 ice cubes.

Blend until combined.

Pour into a rocks glass and serve with a lime wedge.

COCONUT CUPCAKE

INSPIRED BY **CRÈME FATALE**

What's pastel blue and gorgeous all over? Crème Fatale! This queen is crashing the cis-tem with one glorious look after another. Her daydreamy turns are fresh from fairy tales and the glittery world of mermaids, witches and cupcakes. Don't get it twisted, though – this queen has something to say and we will be quiet while the queen is speaking! This polar blue concoction needed to embody the cutesy pastel tones of Crème, while also packing a punch. And only a martini can do that! Shake over ice (shimmying encouraged but not essential), pour into a martini glass and serve. And we mean SERVE.

INGREDIENTS

25ml (⅚fl oz) white rum

5ml (⅛fl oz) blue Curaçao

100ml (3⅓fl oz) coconut milk

METHOD

Pour the white rum, blue Curaçao and coconut milk into a cocktail shaker with ice and shake vigorously until combined.

Pour the mix into a chilled martini glass to serve.

GAINS GAINS GAINS

INSPIRED BY **MISS TOTO**

Welcome to the haus of Gaynz, where every day is leg day. The bodybuilding Barbie of Chicago, Miss Toto Clermont Dion is like no other queen in the contemporary drag scene. She is, of course, partial to a set of dumbbells but is also an international DJ and philanthropist, raising huge amounts of money for the Black Lives Matter movement and countless other causes. But, of course, this cocktail had to play up Miss Toto's strengths... which just so happens to be her strength! So, put everything in a blender... and boom! You've got a boozy protein shake to fuel your night out on the town!

INGREDIENTS

25ml (⅞fl oz) dark rum

200ml (6¾fl oz) whole milk

2 scoops of protein powder

½ banana

1 tbsp smooth peanut butter

To serve

Extra banana slices

Drizzle of smooth peanut butter (optional)

METHOD

Put all the ingredients into a blender and blend to combine. Transfer the mixture to a highball glass and serve with a straw.

Finish with extra banana slices and a drizzle of peanut butter if desired.

BLACK CANDY

INSPIRED BY **LIQUORICE BLACK**

Do not adjust your sets, this monochrome marvel lives in a black-and-white world! She oozes timeless glamour and pulls off chic showgirl like no one else. Liquorice Black is part of Manchester's thriving drag scene, which is known for its attitude, originality and community. This cocktail simply had to be strong, sweet and flavoured with the distinct taste of liquorice. The Black Candy cocktail is finished with a liquorice stick – stop for a mid-drink nibble and chew over how none of us will ever be as fabulous as THE Liquorice Black.

INGREDIENTS

25ml (⅞fl oz) gin

12.5ml (⅜fl oz) black sambuca

12.5ml (⅜fl oz) blackcurrant cordial

Soda water, to top up

To serve

Liquorice stick

METHOD

Pour the gin, sambuca and blackcurrant cordial
into a rocks glass and stir to combine.

Fill with ice and top up with soda water.
Serve with a liquorice stick.

DIVA LAS VEGAS

INSPIRED BY **HOT CHOCOLATE**

Céline Dion, Britney Spears, Janet Jackson, Cher...
Who is the real Las Vegas Diva in residence? It's
the world's best Tina Turner impersonator, and
all-round drag legend, Hot Chocolate, of course!
Larry Edwards (aka Hot Chocolate) really is an icon
of the drag world. They've appeared in numerous
stage shows, films and TV shows, and were even
given the keys to the city of Las Vegas for their work
in promoting the hospitality industry of the area.
In tribute to Larry, we decided to heavily lean into
their drag persona namesake and create a boozy hot
chocolate, simply adding Jack Daniel's Tennessee
whiskey for a loving nod to Tina Turner's home
state. It's the perfect blend of Tina and Larry!

METHOD

Heat the milk then stir through the hot chocolate
powder and whisk until frothy. Stir in the Jack Daniel's
and transfer to a heatproof mug or glass.

Top with whipped cream and a dusting of
cocoa powder to serve.

INGREDIENTS

200ml (6¾fl oz) whole milk

3 tbsp hot chocolate powder

25ml (⅝fl oz) Jack Daniel's

To serve

Whipped cream

Cocoa powder

SICKLY SWEET

INSPIRED BY **BIQTCH PUDDIN'**

The winner of season 2 of *The Boulet Brothers' Dragula*, Biqtch Puddin' has an Emmy nomination under her belt and was instrumental in organising the first digital drag shows in response to the COVID-19 lockdowns, providing a safety net for drag artists the world over. Biqtch Puddin' has truly cemented her place in drag history. We could have gone full filth and used Biqtch's performance as a mop bucket-drinking janitor as the reference point for this cocktail, but we saved you the horror of that and decided to play with her delicious surname instead – phew!

INGREDIENTS

Toffee sauce

25ml (⅝fl oz) Kahlua

25ml (⅝fl oz)
Irish cream liqueur (liquor)

25ml (⅝fl oz) vodka

To serve

Soft toffee or caramel

METHOD

Drizzle toffee sauce into the bottom of a martini glass and up the sides. Pour the Kahlua, Irish cream liqueur (liquor) and vodka into a cocktail shaker with ice. Shake vigorously until combined.

Pour the mix into the martini glass and finish by placing a soft toffee or caramel on the rim of the glass.

POLISH PRINCESS

INSPIRED BY **ALEXIS SAINT-PETE**

Embracing the hyper-sexualised, the powerful, the intimidating, the standout divas of our generation, Alexis crafted her drag persona from the female icons of early 2000s pop music. And it's not just a façade – Alexis is all of those things, but her aesthetics and style of performing are just one side of this Polish sex siren. Alexis is a kind soul with a warm, loving nature and this was the inspiration behind the flavours in this sweet cocktail. She's naughty, she's nice, she's a little bit Alexis!

INGREDIENTS

50ml (1⅔fl oz) Żubrówka vodka

150ml (5fl oz) apple juice

½ tsp honey

¼ tsp ground cinnamon

To serve

Cinnamon stick

METHOD

Put the Zubrówka vodka, apple juice, honey and cinnamon in a cocktail shaker with ice and shake vigorously until combined.

Pour the mix into a rocks glass filled with ice and finish with a cinnamon stick to serve.

GREEN WITH ENVY

INSPIRED BY **ENVY PERU**

Your mum hates her, but your dad adores her! Envy Peru is a trilingual model, actor, makeup artist, TV presenter, pageant winner and winner of *Drag Race Holland,* season 1... It's hard not to be envious of her, to be honest. Instead of serving you some advocaat or a Dutch beer, we decided to step away from the Netherlands for a moment and embrace Envy's Peruvian roots. Adding green juice along with the lime juice, we've added a twist to the national cocktail of Peru and Chile, the Pisco Sour. Why try to fight the envy when you can drink it in?

INGREDIENTS

25ml (⅚fl oz) lime juice

25ml (⅚fl oz) green juice

25ml (⅚fl oz) pisco

1 egg white

METHOD

Pour the lime juice, green juice, pisco and egg white into a cocktail shaker with ice and shake vigorously until combined.

Pour the mix into a chilled Nick & Nora glass to serve.

SCREW YOU

INSPIRED BY **BIMINI BON BOULASH**

Where do we start with BBB?! Model, musician, author, club promoter... the list goes on! This Norwich icon sashayed onto our screens in season 2 of *RuPaul's Drag Race UK*, stole our hearts, and never gave them back. Their forward-thinking drag looks cemented them as a fashion icon and their (completely endearing) IDGAF attitude made us feel like we could all be their mate. This cocktail had to be a little bit naughty and a little bit nice. Top with a maraschino cherry and repeat after us... 'the nipples are the eyes of the face'.

INGREDIENTS

25ml (⅝fl oz) vodka

150ml (5fl oz) blood orange juice

3 dashes of Angostura bitters

To serve

Maraschino cherry

METHOD

Fill a rocks glass with ice and add the vodka and orange juice. Stir to combine.

Add the Angostura bitters and top with a maraschino cherry to serve.

TIP For a mocktail version, omit the Angostura bitters and try substituting the vodka for a non-alcoholic vodka alternative.

PARIS RUNWAY

INSPIRED BY **NICKY DOLL**

Lights, cameras, RUNWAY! It's couture week in Paris and Nicky Doll is the belle of every show, from Cristóbal Balenciaga to Christian Dior. Her knowledge of fashion, style and beauty is unrivalled and she possesses an aura only understood by the Paris elite. With a slight twist on a classic French cocktail, this velvety mix is served in a coupette glass with a lemon twist. Don't break a nail, now – this is class in a glass! *À votre santé!*

INGREDIENTS

50ml (1⅔fl oz) apricot brandy

25ml (⅝fl oz) Cointreau

25ml (⅝fl oz) lemon juice

To serve

Lemon twist

METHOD

Pour the apricot brandy, Cointreau and lemon juice into a cocktail shaker with ice and shake vigorously until combined.

Pour the mix into a chilled coupette glass and top with a lemon twist to serve.

DRAG-
INSPIRED
COCKTAIL
PARTY
PLAYLIST

SOME MUSICAL INSPIRATION FOR YOUR
NEXT COCKTAIL PARTY – SHAKE UP YOUR FAVOURITE
DRAG-INSPIRED COCKTAILS AND GET THIS PLAYLIST
ON TO GET THE PARTY STARTED!

I'M COMING OUT DIANA ROSS

IT'S RAINING MEN THE WEATHER GIRLS

GIMME! GIMME! GIMME! (A MAN AFTER MIDNIGHT) ABBA

I WILL SURVIVE GLORIA GAYNOR

TOXIC BRITNEY SPEARS

CONFIDENT DEMI LOVATO

BITCH BETTER HAVE MY MONEY RIHANNA

BARBIE GIRL AQUA

AIN'T NO OTHER MAN CHRISTINA AGUILERA

GIRLS JUST WANT TO HAVE FUN CYNDI LAUPER

IF I COULD TURN BACK TIME CHER

RAIN ON ME ARIANA GRANDE AND LADY GAGA

TURN THE BEAT AROUND GLORIA ESTEFAN

I WANNA DANCE WITH SOMEBODY WHITNEY HOUSTON

WHAT'S LOVE GOT TO DO WITH IT TINA TURNER

LET'S GET LOUD JENNIFER LOPEZ

STOP! IN THE NAME OF LOVE THE SUPREMES

I'M SO EXCITED THE POINTER SISTERS

INTO THE GROOVE MADONNA

RESPECT ARETHA FRANKLIN

LOVE ON TOP BEYONCÉ

I'M EVERY WOMAN CHAKA KHAN

MURDER ON THE DANCEFLOOR SOPHIE ELLIS-BEXTOR

BORN THIS WAY LADY GAGA

HOW WILL I KNOW WHITNEY HOUSTON

9 TO 5 DOLLY PARTON

TEENAGE DREAM KATY PERRY

COOL FOR THE SUMMER DEMI LOVATO

MAN! I FEEL LIKE A WOMAN! SHANIA TWAIN

INTO YOU ARIANA GRANDE

GOOD AS HELL LIZZO

WRECKING BALL MILEY CYRUS

CAN'T GET YOU OUT OF MY HEAD KYLIE MINOGUE

DISCO INFERNO TINA TURNER

SPICE UP YOUR LIFE SPICE GIRLS

HOW TO MAKE A LEMON TWIST

A lemon twist is a corkscrew-shaped piece of lemon peel, and is a fun addition to any cocktail – it's simple to make but looks really impressive! You can make some twists in advance of your cocktail party and store them in an airtight container in the fridge for up to three days. You can also make lime or orange twists using the same method.

TIP

Using a room temperature lemon means that the peel will be more malleable and easier to form into the corkscrew shape.

METHOD

1 Using a sharp knife, cut a round slice of lemon about ¼ inch (6mm) thick.
2 Slice through one side of the peel.
3 Gently pull the lemon flesh and pith away from the peel, using your knife or your fingers.
4 If necessary, trim any additional white pith from the peel – pith will allow the twist to hold its shape, but too much will add bitterness to your cocktail.
5 If you want your twist to look perfect, trim the edges of the peel with a knife to form a uniform width.
6 Twist the peel around a long skewer (like a chopstick or a straw) to form a corkscrew shape. It should naturally hold its shape.
7 Serve with your favourite cocktail and enjoy!

INDEX BY SPIRIT

GENERAL INDEX

ABOUT THE AUTHORS

RAJA GEMINI won season three of *RuPaul's Drag Race* and was a runner up in 2022's *RuPaul's Drag Race All Stars: All Winners* competition. A connoisseur of all things divine, Raja has released her own Sauvignon Blanc, 'Wine and Complain'.

GREG BAILEY is a drag photographer, creative consultant and writer based in Brighton, UK. He is co-host of the *Alright Darling* podcast and author of the book and zine *Alright Darling?*, a glorious examination of the contemporary drag scene.

ALICE WOOD is a recipe developer and food and drink stylist based in London. Alice has developed an otherworldly ability to mix a cocktail in the spirit of a drag queen.

ABOUT THE ILLUSTRATOR

RUTH MOOSBRUGGER is an illustrator who has worked for *Vogue*, *GQ* and *Glamour* magazines. Ruth uses collage to create illustrations that mix a host of different influences, from leaves to lipstick, money to microphones.

ACKNOWLEDGEMENTS

Thank you to Bella and Andrew at Quarto for asking me to do this project; I loved brainstorming ideas with you and helping you bring the concept through to fruition. It was also a joy working with the genius mixologist Alice Wood to create these camp cocktails, and have Ruth Moosbrugger's beautiful illustrations to make each cocktail look as delicious and flamboyant as they could be. This book was so fun to be a part of that I couldn't just keep it to myself. I'd like to thank my best Judy and my *Alright Darling* podcast co-host Daniel Leo Stanley for coming on board to help me bring some of these recipe introductions to life by injecting his witty writing skills into a handful of the drag performer write ups.

First published in 2023 by White Lion Publishing,
an imprint of Quarto.
1 Triptych Place
London, SE1 9SH

www.Quarto.com

Introduction on pages 8–11 and recipe introductions by
Greg Bailey, except for pages 70, 73, 82, 85, 97, 100, 110
and 112, by Daniel Leo Stanley
Recipes by Alice Wood
Text © 2023 Quarto Publishing
Foreword © 2023 Raja Gemini
Illustrations © 2023 Ruth Moosbrugger

Images sourced from: Brusheezy.com, Pexels.com,
Rawpixel.com, Unsplash.com, Vecteezy.com

A catalogue record for this book is available from the
British Library.

ISBN 978 0 7112 8449 4
Ebook ISBN 978 0 7112 8881 2

Publisher: Jessica Axe
Commissioning Editor: Andrew Roff
Editor: Bella Skertchly
Designer: Renata Latipova

Printed in China